MW00977081

Happy Robot zd3

By Joy Cowley

Illustrated by Joe L. Lai and Alan Wang

Dominie Press, Inc.

Publisher: Christine Yuen
Editor: John S. F. Graham
Designer: Lois Stanfield
Illustrator: Joe L. Lai
3D Artist: Alan Wang

Published by:

ᡍ Dominie Press, Inc.

1949 Kellogg Avenue
Carlsbad, California 92008 USA

www.dominie.com

Paperback ISBN 0-7685-1081-3
Library Bound Edition ISBN 0-7685-1494-0
Printed in Singapore by PH Productions Pte Ltd
2 3 4 5 6 PH 04 03

Table of Contents

Chapter One
The Robot Janitor 4

Chapter Two
Ready for Anything 8

Chapter Three
These Look a Bit Odd 13

Chapter Four
Three Whizz-Bangs 19

Chapter Five
A Shining Silver Whatsit 23

Chapter Six
Tin Pawprints! 28

Chapter One
The Robot Janitor

ZD3, the robot janitor,
was programmed
to be happy and helpful.
But her happy program was bigger
than her helpful program,
so she sometimes made mistakes.
When her robot dog, K9,
tried to help,
he usually made things worse.

"Never mind. You're a fine dog,"
ZD3 would say.

ZD3 and K9 worked
at Cherry Pie Elementary School.
Every morning,
they flew to the school
on ZD3's jet bike, *zip, zip, zip.*
K9 sat on the front, *yip, yip, yip.*
A bag of fixing tools
was tied on the back.

All day, ZD3 cleaned the school.
She tried to fix things
that were broken,
and she tried to make the teachers
and the children happy.
In ZD3's happy program,
there were two thousand songs
and a million smiles.
That meant a lot of happiness
at Cherry Pie Elementary School.

Chapter Two

Ready for Anything

It was a fine, hot morning.
ZD3 was getting ready for work,
polishing her arms and legs
and oiling her eyelids.
While she was busy, K9
put his tin nose in the fixing bag.

The bag had some spare parts
that were old and dusty.
K9 tossed everything out
and then filled the bag
with new fixing things.
He put in some *hoo-dackies*,
some *whizz-bangs*, a *whatsit*,
and a great enormous star buster.
Now they were ready for anything!
thought K9, wagging his tin tail.

As they zipped along on the jet bike,
K9 barked happily while ZD3 sang:

Old MacDonald had a jet bike.
Ee-i, ee-i, o!
And on that jet bike
she had a robot.
Ee-i, ee-i, o!
With a clang, clang here and a clang,
clang there.
Here a clang, there a clang,
everywhere a clang, clang.
Old MacDonald had a jet bike.
Ee-i, ee-i, o!

When they landed
at Cherry Pie Elementary School,
Miss Crust, the principal,
was on the steps,
gasping and wringing her hands.
"Oh, help us please, Miss ZD3!
We are as hot as hot can be!
The air conditioning
has broken down!"

ZD3 replied,

"Miss Crust, have no fear.

Your helpful janitor is here.

Your school will soon be cool.

K9, give me my fixing bag."

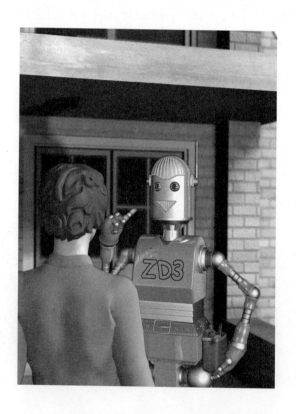

Chapter Three

These Look a Bit Odd

Miss Crust watched
while the janitor worked.

With great care,
ZD3 took the broken *hoo-dackies*
out of the air-conditioning unit
and put new ones in.

"These look a bit odd,"
said ZD3 to K9.

K9 wagged his tail,
which squeaked slightly.

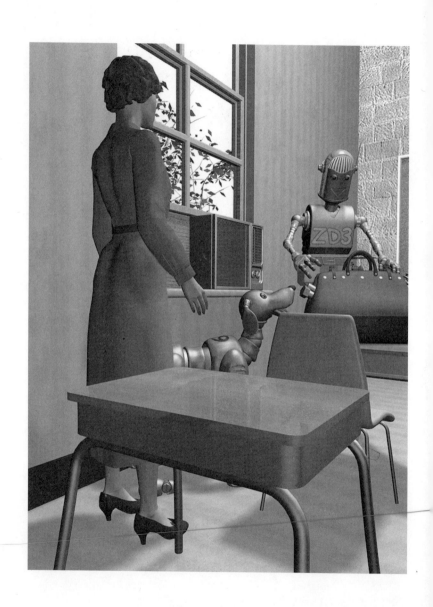

"It's fixed, Miss Crust," ZD3 said,
reaching for the switch.
"Your school will now be cool."
She pulled down the switch.

The air-conditioning unit
rattled and rumbled,
shivered and shook,
then POW!

It fired red Ping-Pong balls
across the room.

Balls bounced off the ceiling.
Balls bounced off the walls.
Balls bounced off Miss Crust,
who cried, "Oh no! Oh no!"

K9's tail stopped wagging.
He crawled under a chair.

ZD3 pushed up the switch,
and the air-conditioning unit
stopped firing Ping-Pong balls.

"I wonder what went wrong?"
said ZD3.

Miss Crust could not answer.
She had a red Ping-Pong ball
in her mouth.

Chapter Four

Three Whizz-Bangs

ZD3 tried again.
She took three *whizz-bangs*
from the fixing bag
and put them in the unit.

"I'm making your school cool,"
she said to the children.

A boy called Sam said,
"Our school is always cool.
The only problem is,
we've got hot air."

"Your problem has been solved,"
said ZD3, closing the fixing bag.
"All we have to do
is turn on the switch."

ZD3 didn't see K9 under the chair
with his tin paws over his tin ears.
She pulled down the switch.

The unit flittered.
The unit fluttered.
The unit fizzed and whizzed
and spluttered.

Then it shot fireworks into the air.
Showers of red sparks!
Streams of green sparks!
Rockets and Roman Candles!
Sparklers and Golden Rain!

"Wow!" cried the children.
"It isn't even the Fourth of July!"

Chapter Five

A Shining Silver Whatsit

"I'll get it right this time."
ZD3 opened her fixing bag
and picked out a brand new
shining silver *whatsit*.

"It looks odd," she said. "In fact,
everything in this bag looks odd."

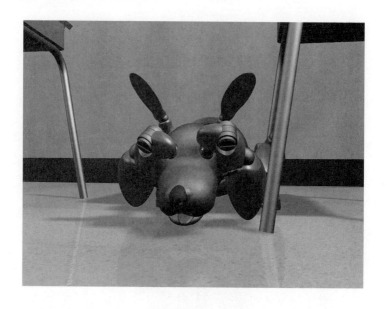

She carefully fitted the silver *whatsit*
into the air-conditioning unit,
while K9 looked the other way.

Miss Crust, who had got rid of
the Ping-Pong ball, said,
"Please do something, ZD3.
This heat is surely killing me."

"At once, Miss Crust!" said ZD3.
"This time, you'll have cool air."

She pulled down the switch.

The air-conditioning unit
splished and sploshed.
It gurgled and sloshed.
Then out shot a fountain
of cold lemonade.

"Oops!" said ZD3. "Another mistake!
K9, have you been meddling
with my fixing bag?"

But K9 was clattering out the door
on his four tin paws,
his tin tail dragging on the floor.

"I'm sorry, Miss Crust," said ZD3.
"I'll try again."

Miss Crust stopped her.
"Let it be, Miss ZD3.
This cold lemonade
looks very good to me."

"Yay!" cried the children,
running with paper cups.
"Cold lemonade on a hot day!"

Chapter Six

Tin Pawprints!

While the school
had a lemonade party,
ZD3 zipped back home
to find the old and dusty spare parts
that had been in her fixing bag.

Ah! There they were on the floor,
with tin pawprints all over them!

When she returned to the school,
it didn't take her long
to clean up the left-over lemonade,
the damp firecrackers,
and the soggy red Ping-Pong balls.
Then, in two wags of a tin dog's tail,
she fixed the air-conditioning unit.
Once more, cool air flowed through
Cherry Pie Elementary School.

"Behold! The air is cold!"
cried Miss Crust.
"Back to class, everyone!"

"Thank you, Miss ZD3!"
the children called.

ZD3 went off to find K9,
who was hiding in the library.
She patted her robot dog.
Clang, clang, clang.
"It's all right, K9," she said.
"You were only trying to help."

K9 wagged his squeaky tail,
and ZD3 gave him a dose of oil.
Then she fitted mower blades
to her feet, and went out
to mow the school lawns.
As she walked around the grass,
she sang a happy song.

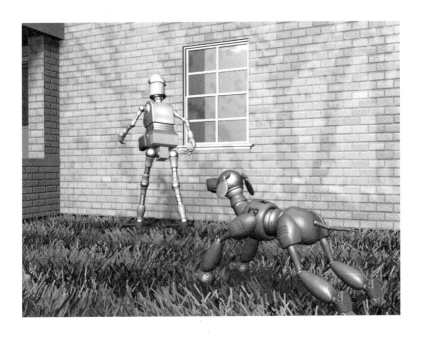

Jingle blades,
Jingle blades,
Jingle all the way.
Being a robot is such fun
on a summer's day.
HEY!

Behind her trotted K9.
He was wondering
what an air conditioner would do
with a great enormous star buster
in it.